Opposites

Hot and Cold

Siân Smith

Raintree is an imprint of Capstone Global Library Limited, a company incorporated in England and Wales having its registered office at 7 Pilgrim Street, London, EC4V 6LB – Registered company number: 6695582

www.raintreepublishers.co.uk
myorders@raintreepublishers.co.uk

Text © Capstone Global Library Limited 2015
First published in hardback in 2014
The moral rights of the proprietor have been asserted.

Edited by Siân Smith, Diyan Leake, and Brynn Baker
Designed by Tim Bond and Peggie Carley
Picture research by Liz Alexander
Production by Victoria Fitzgerald
Originated by Capstone Global Library Ltd
Printed and bound in China

ISBN 978 1 406 28302 0
18 17 16 15 14
10 9 8 7 6 5 4 3 2 1

British Library Cataloguing in Publication Data
A full catalogue record for this book is available from the British Library.

Acknowledgements
We would like to thank the following for permission to reproduce photographs: Alamy: Food for Thought, 15, imagebroker, 18; Corbis: Vincenzo Lombardo/Robert Harding World Imagery, 12; Getty Images: YinYang, 20 right; Shutterstock: 3445128471, 17, Africa Studio, 4, 22a, front cover right, Denis Kuvaev, 11, Evlakhov Valeriy, 21 left, gorillaimages, 6, HandmadePictures, 21 right, Janis Smits, 14, kamilpetran, front cover left, Kaponia Aliaksei, 16, Nuvola, 10, Ramona Heim, 5, 23b, Smit, 8, back cover bottom, stockcreations Evlakhov Valeriy, 20 left, Stuart Monk, 9, Tyler Olson, 13, Yuriy Kulik, 7, back cover top

Every effort has been made to contact copyright holders of material reproduced in this book. Any omissions will be rectified in subsequent printings if notice is given to the publisher.

Contents

Hot and cold

The ice is **cold**.

The fire is **hot**.

The snow is cold.

The Sun is hot.

This snowman is cold.

This potato is hot.

This frost is cold.

This food is hot.

An igloo is cold.

A hairdryer is hot.

The freezer is cold.

The pan is hot.

This drink is hot.

This drink is cold.

Is this drink hot or cold?

The drink is hot.

Hot and cold quiz

Which of these things are hot?

Which of these things are cold?

Answers on page 22

Picture glossary

cold low temperature

hot high temperature

Index

Answers to questions on pages 20 and 21

Sausages are hot.

Ice cream is cold.

Notes for teachers and parents

Building background:

Ask: When have you been hot (in the summer, in the bath, on holiday, after running)? When have you been cold (in the winter, in the snow, in the rain)? Which did you like best?

AFTER READING

Recall and reflection:

Is ice hot or cold? Is fire hot or cold? What happens when ice melts? Is it hot or cold? What happens when a fire goes out? Is it hot or cold?

Sentence knowledge:

Ask children to look at pages 6 and 7. How many sentences are there on each page?

Word knowledge (phonics):

Encourage children to point at the word *cold* on any page. Sound out the four phonemes in the word *c/o/l/d*. Ask the child to sound out each phoneme as they point at the letters and then blend the sounds together to make the word *cold*. Challenge them to say some words that rhyme with *cold* (bold, gold, hold, sold).

Word recognition:

Ask children to point at the word on page 8 that is made of two words (snowman).

AFTER-READING ACTIVITIES

Label two boxes, one hot and one cold. Cut out pictures of hot and cold things (ice, snow, snowman, fridge, freezer, Sun, fire, heater). Ask children whether the items are hot or cold. Then ask children to put the pictures in the correct boxes.

In this book

Topic

hot and cold

Sentence stems

1. This ___ is ___.
2. Is ___ ___ or ___?
3. It is ___.
4. A ___ is ___.

High-frequency words

a

an

and

are

is

of

or

the

these

this

which